Four Hundred & Four In A Bed

Written and illustrated by

Penny Edgar

The Perils and Pleasures of B&B Life

For my family.. who are nearly as mad as I am.

I love you all *so* much.

Contents

Forward

Welcome to the mysterious, multifarious, mattress crunching world of Bed & Breakfast!

Not yet a major feature film narrated by our nation's favourite animal lover Sir David Attenborough, but considering all the gorillas involved it really should be.

This little book is a light-hearted and somewhat irreverent account of running a B&B from home. I hope to show you exactly what you need to do in order to be a success.

Every story and anecdote you are about to read is (almost) entirely true. Most are my own taken from my years of B&Bing, but there are one or two that happened to friends of mine. Rather them than me as you will find out.

What happened (and still happens) to me might inspire you so much that you too will end up giving it a go.

I hope you enjoy reading these stories as much as I did living through them. I wouldn't have changed a thing.

Penny

Four Hundred And Four In A Bed

In the beginning

Who would have thought changing bedsheets and cleaning loos could be so entertaining? Who would have thought cooking endless breakfasts and ironing miles of bedding could be so much *fun!*

Actually, it's not.

But do not despair, for other things *are* pretty funny.

Anywhere there are people eating, sleeping, toileting and fornicating is going to be amusing.

It can also be mildly scary and sometimes just downright weird, but before we get into telling stories about guests and what they get up to, let's be boring and practical first.

What does a person actually need in order to run a Bed & Breakfast? What are the basic guide lines?

Well, unlike everything else in this book, running a B&B is not all black and white.

B&B hosts need to be adaptable, indomitable, flexible and chameleonesque. In fact anything *but* black and white.

The ever-changing nature of this business will keep you wearing more hats than Queen Elizabeth II (that's an awful lot of hats). You will need to develop the patience of Saint Frances (a very patient person, especially around kids and animals) and better skills of diplomacy than Boris Johnson. Actually not him - he's complete rubbish.

To be truthful I can't think of anyone who doesn't offend somebody, so we'll simply leave it that you need to be as nice as you can, most of the time.

B&Bing is a challenging and tricky career, I'm not got to pretend otherwise.

And why is it tricky?

Because *people* are tricky that's why, and Bed & Breakfast hospitality is all about *them.*

At this point I should make it quite clear that this book illustrates the delights and delirium of running a beautiful little bijou B&B from home, and not to be confused with a Hotel or Guest House.

I'm not dissing Premier Inns or swanky five star hotels, they all have their place, and some people I'm closely related to wouldn't stay anywhere else.

But B&Bs are different creatures altogether and shouldn't be confused with impersonal, corporate and yes dare I say it boring, samey spaces where you could be in any town, in any city, in any country on the face of the earth. Same décor, same menu, even the same feckin' parking spaces.

So, so dull.

B&Bs are unique and special. You will never find the same one twice.

They are different because they are run by different people with different ideas and ways of doing things. The joy of it is, a guest can never know how it's going to be until they get there. It's like one of those lucky dips at the fair. It's a gamble with a bit more than a quid, but if the guest hits the jackpot they'll never regret it.

Believe it or not, real, live human relationships are formed in this cosy little world of ours, no matter how brief and no matter how quirky, and believe you me they can get quirky.

But before we get to all that, let's get down to the business end of it shall we? Let's take a look at the nuts and bolts of it.

First we need to address the pluses and minuses, the pros and cons, and the perils and pitfalls of turning your life over to Bed &Breakfast.

On the plus side, how would it feel to work from home?

Imagine never having to do the daily commute, find a parking space or buy a suit? No more office politics, bitchy co-workers and rubbish pay rises. No more embarrassing Christmas Parties!

Doesn't sound so bad does it?

Maybe you are a little hard up, short of cash, a bit strapped. Most of us are pretty well squeezed these days and could do with a little extra.

B&Bing could be the answer.

Do you have a spare room gathering dust? What about your loft? What about the kids' rooms? Not if there's a 7 year old in residence because it's very unkind to evict primary school children, but if the big ones have moved out to shack up elsewhere (don't worry, they'll be back) wouldn't it make sense to have those empty spaces working for you?

How would it feel to know that while you sleep your property assets are making you lots of lovely money?

It's a bit like being The Duke of Westminster, only on a slightly smaller scale.

In this job you are free to be yourself, and in fact the more you are yourself, the better you will do.

Generally speaking, people really do like other people.

They especially like them if they are authentic, kindly and genuine. When you bring people into your home it is important they feel welcome and not that you're just in it for the money (even if you are), so remember..

False friendliness makes folks nervous. We've all had that uncomfortable feeling when someone is being nice to our face, while at the same time trying

to get one over on us, pull the wool over our eyes –
or even stab us in the back.

It's not nice.

Your guests will appreciate you being your true,
honest self, even if you're so knackered you can't be
arsed to make them a cup of tea.

There's something very disarming about being real.
People get drawn to it – it fascinates them.

Honesty breaks down barriers like nothing else, so
in the end everyone knows exactly who they are.
There's no green slimy resentful monsters lurking in
dark shadows, waiting to leap out of the wardrobe
and scare the crap out of you. When we are our true

selves everyone gets to have a good old comfy time and that's what it's all about.

In this job you work in your own space, in your own time, and do as much or as little as you want - when you want.

You can take four weeks off in July, disappear to the sun from November to March, take as much time as you like.

You can shut the shop and bugger off to Spain without having to grovel to the boss, plead with your co-workers or negotiate strenuously with your partner.

You are answerable to no one. You are free..

Sound like a dream job? Well in a sense it is but I would suggest you read on to find out how best to avoid this dream job becoming your worst nightmare.

It could happen.

Being Realistic

The first question you must ask yourself before hanging out the "Vacancies" sign is simple.

Do you really have the space in your home (and your life), for complete and utter strangers?

It's a basic question, but if not properly considered could lead to hugely expensive and protracted therapy sessions in the future.

If you happen to be a little short on company, this could be the answer. It is after all an extraordinarily handy way to meet new people. You never need to leave the house - everyone comes to you!

It's worth bearing in mind however, there are no filtration systems in place. Your guests are not interviewed first. No one gets to fill in any questionnaires regarding compatibility.

It's not at all like Match.com.

You don't get to *choose* these people, they simply turn up.

By the time they are ringing the doorbell it's far too late to say "Sorry. I can't accommodate people with snakes in their hair and hamsters down their trousers" (Not a true story)

Are you prepared to be prepared, and accept whatever you get?

It helps in some small way to know whoever and whatever your guests might be, they will still be bringing their money with them.

Yet, as we all know, money isn't everything and the 'wrong' guests can actually end up *costing* you money.

Next you might want to consider if your house is set up for it?

By this I mean is the layout workable for a bed and breakfast?

For example, if guests have to walk through your kitchen to get to the lav there could be issues ahead. Especially if they have a high fibre diet and enjoy a daily curry.

Worse still they might need to walk through your lounge room to get to their bedroom every night.

On the way it could be only too easy for them to stop off and join you in the evening for drinks, nibbles and a natter.

This could seriously eat into your profits as well as your spinach puffs. Not to mention compromise your viewing schedule.

Guests remarkably easily make themselves at home, plump up your cushions, change the channel, help themselves to another glass of wine.

People soon forget you are not actually their mother.

The house set-up needs to work for them *and* for you, or it won't work at all.

You might have to grit your teeth and spend some money on alterations and improvements. Always painful I know, but what is the saying? 'You've got to speculate to accumulate'.

It's not exactly speculation of course, its *investment*, because whatever you spend will be spent on your own property and therefore hopefully add to its long term value. Your children would much prefer you to do that than blow their inheritance on a Greek experience, however tempting he/she may be.

It's the 21st century and modern people have modern standards. Nowadays guests expect to get a room AND an ensuite.

Gone are the days when folks were happy to scuttle down the corridor for a tiddle. Now they want privacy and the convenience of a handy convenience.

A shower in the ensuite is quite acceptable but the addition of a bath will elevate your guests' experience.

Guests love a bit of luxurious lounging, and you can charge a bit more for that too.

Of course, do bear in mind the bloody thing will need cleaning.

Don't forget to install a beast of an extractor in the ensuite.

How ever much someone might love their other half, it's a big ask to expect them to be ok with questionable personal fragrances if they can't open the feckin' windows.

If you have limited space in the bathroom try hanging a huge wall to wall mirror.

This gives the illusion of doubling the size of the room, and also means guests get to see themselves having a wee. People appreciate little things like that.

The bedroom itself must be big enough to accommodate two large humans (size matters when it comes to comfortable arrangements), a wardrobe, tea and coffee making facilities, bedside tables with lamps and the ubiquitous tv. If you can get in a couple of chairs and a small table so much the better. A luggage stool is always appreciated and saves your freshly painted window cills from being trashed by a couple of old bags.

Then the big B. The most important thing of all.

The Bed.

It's going to see some action I'm not going to lie, so essentially it needs to be well built.

Guests tend to make the very most of their time away from home and a sturdy frame will help withstand the creaking and squeaking which might disturb you and your other guests.

While we are about it, make sure your bedroom doors fit as snugly as possible. Sound carries further at night.

It is impossible to buy a bed that is too big. Bigger is much, much better. If you work on the assumption that your guests will all be super-sized, you won't go far wrong.

There are few things quite so depressing as watching two larger than life guests sit down on the end of an inadequate bed as the whole thing gives up hope and sinks like the Titanic into the shag-pile.

A big bed means you and your guests will sleep better at night. It also means more kilometres of ironing for you, but we'll address that knotty nugget later.

Have you got double glazing in your house? If you are in town or somewhere that gets a bit chilly, you will definitely be needing it.

Even if the ear-splitting noise outside isn't coming from you revving your grandmother's motorbike at 5am or having a massive vodka fuelled row with your best friend, the blame for your guests' rotten night will fall onto you.

You cannot ever guarantee your guests an undisturbed night, but you can at least put some obvious provision in place. Double glazing and making sure your curtains are thick enough to stop the street lights blazing through the windows are some of those things.

Heating for the house must be more than adequate.

You won't get away with a wheezing calor gas stove in the hall and a grubby, sticky dimplex glued to the bathroom wall. Guests don't like freezing their nuts off and having to pay for it.

Put a tidy little electric heater in the room for emergencies but turn the central heating thermostat up a notch and keep the goosebumps, and complaints, at bay.

You might for example get some expats arrive from Malaysia on the UK's hottest day in years. They check-in quite happily but shortly afterwards you find they are in their room turned blue and literally shivering with the cold. Remember to keep extra duvets and blankets for those who have gone soft whilst living abroad.

Some folks are the opposite and they are hot people. They will strip the bed immediately and throw open the windows allowing the unseasonably cold winds to find their way in to every nook and cranny of your cosy little home.

In these instances you will just have to put on your woolly gloves, wear a bobble hat, dig out that hot water bottle and go to bed.

You might look a bit like a market stall holder at Christmas, but no one will ever know.

And look on the bright side – no heating for the hot ones will save you money for the cold ones.

A word about décor.

Personal taste varies like avocados so it's tempting to play it safe.

But I say "Neigh!" (or is it "Nay!"?)

Magnolia and taupe are two soul destroying, mind sapping colours you will find in those hotels I was talking about earlier. Miles and miles of beige corridors stretching out into a desperate, bleak and mundane future where nothing interesting ever happens.

In your B&B you can do what you like. Your décor choices declare who you are, so be bold! Unless you are really boring in which case magnolia is fine.

There is, however, a line to be drawn between extremes of Gothic Castle/Cher's Boudoir type declaration and whimsical/sickly/pink vomit declaration.

I would suggest somewhere in the middle (but not a boring middle).

If it's too exciting your guests will only go crazy, swing off the chandeliers, throw a saddle over the luggage stool and ride that sucker till morning and you will have to clear up the mess. But if it's too pink hearts, unicorns and candy floss you will get roasted in the reviews on Tripadvisor.

"Can't believe we had to sleep in a *Barbie* room! Bleurgh! I'll never get over it!"

Choose a feature colour and dress your rooms around it. It a fun thing to do and will give your guests something to think about and talk to you about in the morning.

Life is way too short to be boring. You won't please all of the people all of the time, but even if they find your taste somewhat challenging, they will still appreciate they've experienced it.

Note: I've never had any visitors be permanently damaged by my walls. At least I don't think I have..

If you think your home is up to it, what about you?

Perhaps you thought running a B&B was just about frying a bit of bacon. Anyone can do that right?

Wrong.

That is one of the greatest Bed and Breakfast myths of all.

Yes, it is about frying acres of bacon (poor old piggy-wigs) but the reality of it is, if your shop is open, this job is a 7 day a week round-the-clock process of which cooking breakfast is but a tiny part.

Are you really happy to give up your home 24/7? Because that is exactly what you will do.

The Nitty Gritty starts here.

The Breakfast

Time to Break the Fast.

Breakfast like a king they say. The most important meal of the day they say. Probably the biggest pain in the backside I say.

Why?

Because your guests will all have a slightly different idea of what the perfect breakfast really is. This means you must cover all basis when it comes to your menu and cooking skills.

To me eggs are the spawn of the devil. (Is it possible to be spawn and egg at the same time? Will ponder on that one).

Poached eggs are the very worst.

As soon as you drop them into the water they turn into ghost eggs and start swirling their multi tendrils like spectres from a horror film. By the time you scoop them out there's bugger-all left except the yellow bit that has turned into Gollum's eye.

You can try to get away with using those little poaching pan jobbies, but I can tell you guests will turn up their noses and make a comment. They expect a superior egg and that just won't do.

Some people cook eggs by wrapping them up in cling film before plunging into the boiling pot of doom. I tried that. The egg stuck like shit to the plastic and made a godawful mess. Stressed me out? I'll say.

My tips for poaching eggs are as follows: Your eggs must be *absolutely* fresh. If not, they will punish you. Secondly the water must be very hot. Let it boil, and just before you put the eggs in, turn it off. Too many bubbles will smash your eggs to pieces. Break the eggs in one by one. Thirdly I wouldn't bother with swirling the water round like a whirlpool. It really doesn't work, in fact I think it makes things worse, and I've never noticed any difference using vinegar no matter what Jamie Oliver says.

A table full of guests will all want something different. It's the law of averages.

It might be Full English all round, but the wretched eggs will be required in umpteen different ways. Boiled, soft poached, hard poached, soft scrambled, firm scrambled, over easy and sunny side up. The bacon will be crispy for one and limp for another. Mushrooms on, mushrooms off. Beans in, beans out.

As a rule of thumb our German friends hate our sausages. Having just said that my German visitors this morning scoffed the whole lot for their breakfast, and apart from saying "It's very English!" (not sure what that means) they were very happy to eat it and have ordered the same again tomorrow.

Our French cousins tend to lean towards more toast and pastries, as do the Italians, but for God's sake get the coffee right.

The Brits will eat anything as long as it's no longer breathing.

You can of course, tell all your fussy egg guests to oeuf off and give them what they get. But if you want those high scores on your doors you will have to perfect your culinary skills. Breakfast-wise anyway.

Some people only want a bit of toast. I love those people. Some only want cereal and a bit of fruit. I love them too. Some want all the above plus cheese, yoghourt and pastries. I don't exactly *love* them but they're alright because there's no cooking involved.

But some people want everything. They will literally devour whatever is within arms' reach, so be careful where you leave the children.

I've had a guest eat all the fruit on the table, all the cheeses, a big bowl of cereal, a full English breakfast, two pots of tea (plus all the little sugar packets) and two rounds of toast, butter and marmalade – and I'm not kidding.

This sort of breakfast costs a lot of money and you might want to think about whether you want to charge extra for your breakfasts.

I don't do it that way. I'm all inclusive. You win some and you lose some, but at least everyone stays friends.

It is a personal choice however, but I reckon it's better to cover the cost of breakfast in advance and include it in your basic price.

After all your guests were happy with the payment when they booked your room. Then you don't have to be the money-grabbing host who stings them when they're starving.

Nowadays you have to be aware of all the allergies, intolerances and sensitivities people have.

Something that's changing rapidly is people's regard for animal welfare.

Remarkable though it may seem, some people actually love cats, dogs *and* piggies - all the same! They don't want to eat any of them! (Piglets are so cute running about oinking, their little ears flapping and their little tails wiggling! Have you seen Babe? It changed everything for me).

Veggie breakfasts are very popular and may I say, easier to wash up. No animal fat clogging up your dishwasher (or your guests' arteries).

Gluten free options are essential these days and easy enough to procure. Milk and dairy alternatives are everywhere, so there's no excuse.

You really must try not to poison your guests.

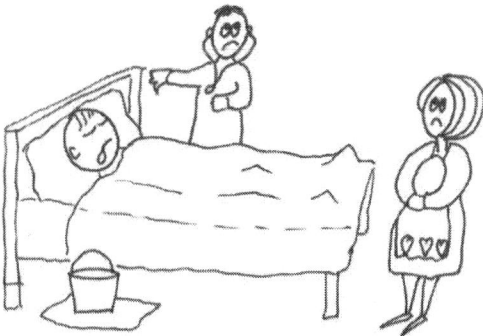

You will soon get to know your breakfast types. People really do fall into groups. I can spot a full English a mile off.

I always keep my fingers crossed it won't be my breakfast that pushes them over the edge.

Handy tip. Know where the nearest defibrillator is located. Hopefully you won't be needing it.

Be prepared.. for anything.

All sorts of unexpected and interesting things can happen when you open up your home to guests.

Some make assumptions, push boundaries and basically 'try it on'. These guests come under the general heading of 'un-wanteds'.

For example, make sure you have a plan should a guest phone you from their room upstairs to ask for help with the shower that doesn't seem to be working.

Give yourself a minute to consider *why* they are telephoning.

It's really not that far to walk downstairs and simply tap on your door to ask for help. If you know the guest upstairs is a single gentleman on his own, you would be foolish indeed not to be expecting something.

If you go up and they answer the door with nought but a hand towel around their waist, it is very important you do not bat an eyelid.

tiny
towel

Remain business like, professional and efficient.

Act as if you encounter such scenes every day of the week and you are neither impressed or otherwise.

Sort the problem (which will probably mean just turning the effing thing on) as quickly as you can and get the hell out of there.

Remember everyone is different and it's not always what you think.

Once a guest has checked in, remember to always double-check to see if they have attached themselves to you in some strange way.

This is because *sometimes* guests will quietly follow you.

This can even be through closed doors, and ones that have the word "Private" in plain sight.

It seems 'Private' might not have the same meaning for some guests as it does for you and I.

For example..

Imagine making the error of thinking your newly wedded octogenarian guests are happily installed upstairs in their room, and you can now switch off and relax.

It's been another very busy day with the B&B and you deserve some time to yourself.

You might make a cup of cocoa, pop on your jimjams and snuggle up in bed watching your favourite tv show.

Suddenly you might notice a small movement at the corner of your eye.

This small movement might turn out to belong to the bride herself who is also watching your favourite tv show whilst standing by your bed.

In these situations it is best not to express any irritation or anger. You never want to frighten newly wedded guests in their eighties.

Just smile benignly when it turns out they simply didn't understand the large rectangular black object fixed to their bedroom wall was in fact a television set.

And realistically, when you think about it, I suppose it must come as no surprise to anyone that the honeymoon couple probably didn't want to do anything other than watch an episode of Eastenders on their wedding night.

I can assure you however that such apparitions appearing when you think you are safe and tucked up in bed with teddy, is enough to frighten the living shit out of anyone.

From time to time you might be asked to do some 'extras'.

As long as you are comfortable with the request this is fine. Never agree to anything you might regret in the morning.

You may have to double up as a taxi driver for instance.

Sometimes guests get in a terrible stew, particularly if they have a wedding to go to, a boat to catch or a university interview to attend. You can help smooth the troubled waters and come out a 5star superstar.

It could be that your dear guests have already booked a cab, but sadly got the wrong time and now are looking to you to rescue them from what could be a calamitous situation.

When this happens, do not panic. Be prepared to leap into action and save the day.

It is a little unfortunate if your car is filthy dirty and covered in seagull poo. It could also be a small issue if it is full of recycling and a sideboard for the charity shop. It could be you need to put a tea towel down on the front seat as the last bum on it belonged to your neighbour's dog. But nevertheless, you will be the hero of the day when you get them, and the lady's hat, to the venue on time.

Sometimes (but not always) they will bung you a few quid for helping out. It's seldom as much as they would have paid a taxi driver, but hey it's all goodwill isn't it?

Things that don't make sense.

There are many things in life that don't make sense.

For example, I often ask myself why is it everything on Earth has a finite life span? Everything gets born, lives and dies – even politicians and lawyers. While the Universe, (of which we are all indisputably a part) is infinite and seemingly timeless and goes on forever. It makes no sense. If we *are* the Universe and the Universe is eternal, why aren't we?

Or then again.. are we?

The other completely senseless thing that irks me every morning when I make a cup of tea, is electricity. What the devil is it?

I asked an electrician once what electricity was and he looked at me as if I was a complete idiot.

"It's what makes the telly work" he said a little patronisingly.

I resisted the temptation to remind him there are many factors that 'make the telly work' but I was ready to accept electricity as being one of them. However, intriguingly, he still hadn't answered my question. We all know what it *does,* I pressed him – but what is it? After a few moments of opening and closing his mouth, he seemed to get a headache and I still don't have the answer.

In B&B world do not be surprised if any senseless, inexplicable, almost creepy things happen from time to time in. It's probably not poltergeists, burglars or Father Christmas. The chances are it's going to be something to do your guests.

You might for instance have left a fascinating newspaper cutting on the window cill of your kitchen, imagining (as you would) such a thing to be more than safe behind the perfectly serviceable door with the perfectly serviceable 'private' sign upon it. After all, who would be interested in such a little thing?

You might therefore, be a little surprised the following day, when going up to tidy your guests' room, that said newspaper cutting has mysteriously made its way upstairs and deposited itself on the bedside table next to their tube of hand-cream.

At least, I think it was hand-cream.

You might then make the decision to leave the cutting where it is and comfort yourself by imagining you must have left it in the breakfast room, not the kitchen after all (but you know bloody well you didn't) and the guests must have picked it up and taken it upstairs after they had their brekkie.

Even more disturbing however is to find, the following day, the newspaper cutting has somehow made its way downstairs again.

Once again it has got itself through the 'private' door, but not back into the kitchen this time. No, it is now in your *own* bedroom, languishing on your *own* bedside table next to your mastercard statement.

Newspaper cuttings are one thing, tampered personal items are another.

You would certainly be forgiven for being a little dismayed or even alarmed to find your favourite lace-up boots with zips on the side (for ease of use) had suffered some kind of interference while you were out.

Knowing as you do you only ever use the zip on the side and *never ever* undo the laces (too much faffing), imagine going into your private rooms and finding one boot as you left it but the other now has its laces trailing like spaghetti on the floor.. and its zip is *up*!

You know what you're like, and you know you never *ever* do the zip up unless you are actually wearing the boot. The other boot is impassive. It stands mutely beside it, zip down, laces up. If only it could talk. That boot was a witness to a crime.

I'm not sure if trying on your Bed & Breakfast host's shoes is technically a crime, but it certainly crosses more than a few personal boundaries. What if they had foot fungus? Ew.

Speaking of footwear, be prepared to see shoes hurled out of a guest bedroom window into the street.

Sometimes this can be amusingly followed by a hearty voice yelling..

"Oi! Wear these you twat!"

Be prepared at a moment's notice to blow up balloons, light candles and remove all traces of alcohol. It's too late to deal with what's already gone down your neck of course, but suck a mint and no one will know.

Feathers in pillows and duvets can be a major issue for those with sensitivities and allergies so make sure you have plenty of synthetic ones to hand. And do not allow your cat/dog/budgerigar/salamander or hairy boyfriend/girlfriend anywhere near the food. Guests really object to finding curlies in their coffee.

Like trusty girl guides and boy scouts we have to be prepared to pick out a horse's hoof and tie a reef knot at any hour of the day.

Well, perhaps not that.

And then there's the weird and wonderful good-old 'empty bed syndrome'.

Where oh where has my dear guest gone?

You could be laying the breakfast table at 7.30am, anticipating hungry guests to be descending from their room at any moment. Suddenly you might be aware of a presence close by. You look up and see, peering blurry eyed through the front window, a strangely familiar but exceedingly dishevelled figure.. in a ballgown.

After checking you are not hallucinating, your major concern in that moment might not necessarily be that your guest will not manage to eat your lovingly prepared breakfast, but rather that they will throw it up all over you should you open the door and let them in.

Very occasionally you might be waiting for guests to come down for a very, very long time. This is because they have checked out in the night...

Handy Tip. Always get the cash up-front.

Selective Hearing

As we shall see later on there are plenty of times when it would help to be already hard of hearing or in possession of a set of earplugs.

Guests have different activities and different noise levels.

Some like to burn the midnight oil and watch tv until 3am, while others leap out of bed as the first fingers of dawn come stealing through the curtains and are out of the house and down the road for their daily yoga practice before you can say "Om"

Some are so quiet you do not know they are there. Mice are far noisier. How these people flush the loo so silently is a mystery.

They will shimmer down for breakfast, missing all the squeaky stairs along the way, and you won't have an inkling they are sitting at the breakfast table waiting for you till you go down with the milk. If these people put the tv on at all it will be so quiet the news readers must be miming.

Frankly I sometimes wonder if they are even breathing.

Other guests are very different. Sometimes I am amazed how loud a telly will go.

It could be it's turned up loud because the guests are yelling at each other.

It's rare that people are having an actual, full-on blazing row, usually they are simply behaving as they always do at home. A partnership disagreement perhaps. A difference of opinion about who gets which side of the bed, that sort of thing.

Some people say they feel lonely if the telly isn't on. They freak out because it's too darn quiet and they think the zombies are coming out.

I kind of get this.

Not the zombie bit, the lonely bit.

I remember only too well, at a time of deep emotional distress, finding my best friends on the telly every morning. There they were, smiling and talking to me in such a friendly and welcoming manner!

Somehow they seemed to understand my problems, even though they couldn't hear a word I was bleating. Through my snot and tears, my wails and travails, they were there for me and I really felt like they cared.

That they were Richard and Judy is frankly a sad reflection of the state of my mental health at the time. But I can tell you if it wasn't for those too lovelies I would still be taking the tablets to this very day.

Sometimes, sadly, guests *are* rowing.

Don't be surprised if a particularly noisy and irksome couple don't go the holiday distance.

You might get a 'heads-up' things aren't going so well when the lady refers to him as "*It* upstairs!" and the gentleman shares with you that "She's off her feckin' head this week!".

If they check out after only two nights, look on the bright side. They won't ask for their money back. They know you've heard the worst of it, and you can always let the room again straight away - and get paid twice.

Bonus!

Housekeeping

Do you like ironing?

Do you like cleaning?

Do you like DIY?

If you do you are obviously a weirdo but having said that this lark should be a piece of cake for you if you do.

If you can't at least tolerate some, or all of these activities you might want to reconsider your career options before going any further.

You can of course get around some of these issues by sending all your washing to the laundry and get a willing and able person in to do the cleaning. But if you want to actually make any money at this, you are going to have to do the work yourself.

Ironing can suck the will to live from any human being in my opinion.

I didn't iron a single thing for over thirty years and was quite happy with the crinkly results. But when you have paying guests they expect the bed to look like no one else has already shagged in it.

There are however some tips to be had to make life a little easier in the ironing department.

For starters don't buy really expensive 1000 thread count, pure white Egyptian Cotton bedding – even from John Lewis.

Yes, they are amazing and feel awesome, but they are a total bitch to iron. It can take a person a whole day to iron one set (two days if you have OCD).

In addition to that, they weigh a ton when damp and hauling them out of the washing machine and onto the ironing board will cripple you in less than a fortnight.

Just remember it is never worth trying to outdo the Dorchester. Some fairly decent stuff will more than do the trick.

Something not too expensive that won't make you cry when a perfectly lovely guest admits he's slept all night with his t-shirt tied round his neck (why would you do that?) and got so sweaty it bled bright red all over the pillows. (It didn't wash out)

Or when a man decides to clean his shoes in bed (why would you do that?) and slops the black boot polish all over the duvet.

(That didn't wash out either)

Just be thankful he didn't spill it on the carpet.

Gratitude is a wonderful thing. It's the little things in life that count.

And the big things.

Now the monster that keeps us all awake at night.

Cleaning.

It is probably the one thing you must get right. You can get away with cold toast at breakfast, but no one is ever going to forgive you for a pube in their porridge.

Unless you are already a professional cleaner you probably have no idea how those little buggers can hide from you. A bathroom will appear to be spotless until you turn out the light and close the door.

Then, like silver fish, they will spill out from under the bath, fall down from the shower rail and sneak out from the cracks around the loo. When you open the door again it will be like a curly carpet in there.

Yes, it's demoralising but you have to be brave. Your next guests will not be expecting to wade through someone else's nose clippings.

A hairy guest will leave enough spare hair to stuff a cushion, so you need a belter of a hoover to make sure you get them all - and always wear your glasses.

People will dribble and spill in the most unlikely places – even on the walls. Never question what is being dribbled or spilled (it will only make you puke), just get on with cleaning it up.

Your carpet will suffer from gawd knows what on it, so at least once a week get down on your hands and knees and scrub those stains.

I need to address the toilet at this point.

Sometimes dark things lurk in toilets.

You might imagine, when you go to clean the room after a person has checked-out, that the good-old flush you've just given the loo will be enough to deliver the guest's final calling card into the sewer system.

How wrong you can be.

Sometimes a knobbly log will *pretend* it's gone, but after a while, when you've gone off elsewhere, will reappear.

It is very important that your next guests don't have the surprise, and may I say the horror, of witnessing the size of your previous guest's poo.

It is not a good way to start anyone's holiday.

It is bad enough for you, and you're prepared and suitably armed, so imagine how horrific it would be for them.

Always return to the scene of the crime at least twice to be certain the ten tonne turd has gone round the bend.

Bins. Lovely bins. Big bins in the bathroom and the bedroom. You will be shocked how much rubbish people can generate in a really short space of time.

You may also be shocked with what people put into a bin, and worst still, make no attempt to conceal.

Usually it's relatively harmless stuff like mountains of sweetie papers, coke bottles and biscuit wrappers. Sometimes there's pill boxes and strange looking tablets that have odd symbols on, and sometimes it's far, far worse.

People will actually leave undisguised, used condoms right there in the bin of a homely little Bed & Breakfast.

Seriously people! Have you no shame?! At least have the courtesy to wrap them up in a tissue.

Sometimes (one must suppose in the heat of the moment) they will have missed the bin altogether and lobbed them directly on to the floor.

Then you have to peel the icky sticky things off the carpet. Ew. Get on your knees again and scrub for your life.

Humans have all sorts of strange habits and bodily functions so for God's sake always use bin liners and don't forget your rubber gloves.

Next up you need towels, towels and more towels. Make sure you have lots and lots of them because they need to be changed every day.

Sounds freakishly excessive I know because no sane person changes them at all until they are filthy and stinky. But this is B&B world and we have to keep things squeaky not reeky.

By the way, unlike sheets it is worth spending a bit more money on towels. Horrible thin ones look awful and are false economy as you will be washing them *a lot.*

You don't need to get the massive bath sheets. Guests are spoilt enough as it is. A large towel and a decent sized hand towel per person is more than adequate.

You have to tumble them in the dryer to soften them, even with fabric softener, or your guests could end up coming down to breakfast looking like they've been beating each other with birch twigs.

In the bathroom you will need to provide plenty of loo paper (naturally), air freshener (of course), shampoo, shower gel and conditioner.

You can get dispensers to fix to the walls or little pots guests can take away with them. They are cleaner, easier and look good. I get eco ones from Out of Eden that don't cost the Earth.

Every little helps.

Everyone wants a cuppa tea, so don't forget the kettle for the guest room.

You can get little ones designed especially for the job so your guests won't be boiling a Burco full of water every time. Mugs (not cups – who uses cups?), a large water bottle, various teas and coffee, sugar and uht milk. Don't forget the non-dairy. A couple of biscuits are always welcome, but don't go mad because people will only eat them.

Put half a dozen hangers in the wardrobe and a hairdryer in the drawer and you're just about there.

Some hosts put in slippers, shower caps and dressing gowns - but what is this? Trump towers?

Being Polite

This might be one of the hardest things of all, especially if someone has been horrid about your exceedingly comfortable arrangements and you are one of those people who has a powerful need to be right *all the time* and are accustomed to having the last word – *so there.* (Not me at all)

In B&B world it is wise to turn the other cheek asap and let things go.

Believe me, having a row is never worth the aggro. After all, these unhappy people are never going to come back and stay with you, so you might as well wave them off to oblivion with a smile.

Okay, maybe not a smile, but anyone can grit their teeth and snarl a bit and that sort of looks like a smile from a distance.

It is extremely rare for a guest to be rude to your face.

However, if they have an issue they might not mention it at the time. They might be as nice as pie as they leave, but once home and it's time to write a review they can turn into cave trolls.

For some people it is far easier to complain about something than be nice. It's like to be complimentary might cost them something.

But remember whatever they say, true words or not, you must maintain your dignity. Never, ever get engaged in a cat fight down a blind alley. It will just make you look like a half-baked twat. Much better to take yourself off, gnaw on your knuckles and phone a friend.

Giving as good as you got will only cost you in the future. Prospective guests read reviews AND responses.

Sometimes guests will push you to the edge while still staying with you.

No matter how many times a guest knocks on your 'privates' to ask for another saucer of milk, keep that smile and a "Bien sur!" at the ready.

Remember these people are paying you and you never want to bite the hand that feeds you.

This gig is all about accommodation. Providing comfortable, clean and tidy accommodation for your guests' comfort, and making sure you accommodate their needs, wants and desires. (Within reason – see previous tiny towel episode).

If a guest should arrive with a suitcase full of medications that need to be kept in your fridge, smile straight away (with a concerned and sympathetic emphasis of course) and explain you need a moment to clear a space.

Sacrificing the future of your delicate and freshly made cream filled pavlova for a guest's pills comes with the territory and when they explain they will need access to your fridge twice a day (and once in the night) for the rest of the week, as always, no grimmace. Smile. "But of course.."

Handy Tip. Don't bother to go to the trouble and expense of buying a mini fridge because a) it won't be big enough, and b) the guests will only complain that it's too noisy, they can't sleep, and use yours anyway.

When it gets a bit too much remember all guests are not permanent fixtures however much they make themselves at home.

They will all be gone in a few days.

Lost in Translation

The chances are you will get people from abroad whose first language is not English.

Do not panic.

Embarrassingly most visitors have a better grasp of the English language than we do. Europeans are clearly far better educated than we are, as a lot of them know at least three languages. I barely know one.

However, it can't hurt to brush up on 'O' level, GCSE or kindergarten French and German, however badly we did at school.

At least it shows we've made an effort, and not relied entirely on shouting.

Bear in mind some visitors are not so well versed in languages as others and this can lead to confusion.

It is important to make sure all your guests understand that they should lock their bedroom doors. If not it could result in some charming Italians forgetting which room is theirs, and accidentally finding themselves trying to explain the error to a bed full of jolly Germans.

While we are about it, never forget to lock your *own* bedroom door too.

I know a hostess who had retired to bed leaving her husband downstairs watching tv. This particular hostess liked to sleep as nature intended, and after a couple of glasses of wine had drifted off into a blissful sleep.

In the wee small hours a movement in the bed next to her woke her up. As she opened her eyes she was startled to see a pair of men's boots perched on the pillow beside her. Knowing they did not belong to her husband, she tentatively pulled back the bed clothes to reveal a shaven headed stranger.

The screams echoed around this town for weeks.

Ordering breakfast can be a little perplexing on occasions when we don't all speak the same language.

But as long as you don't dish up bacon to a vegan or mashed avocado to a raging carnivore, it's rarely a cause for a refund.

Remember also that many of us have to cope with other difficulties. People can be hard of hearing, and some are quite deaf.

If you should get the chance to learn some sign language I can tell you it is really appreciated. Ask your grandchildren to teach you (assuming you have some – if not borrow someone else's) because they often know quite a bit of Makaton.

Fortunately, what needs to be understood usually gets to be understood with the universal language of arm waving, pointing and smiling.

We are all human after all and most of our needs are pretty much the same.

Patience and Personal Power

Patience, as we know, is a virtue and you will be needing some.

Guests will push you and pull you and some will even try to pulverise you.

Saying they will arrive at 4pm and finding them hanging on the doorbell four hours early, while the bed is barely cold from the last guests and you are still scrubbing the pebble-dash off the loo, is a test in forbearance, patience and understanding.

Sometimes they do the other thing and fail to arrive till the wee small hours and that can try the patience of the most saintly amongst us.

Arrivals are one thing, departures are another.

Sometimes they just don't want to leave.

If you make the breakfast room too comfortable they will hang around in there for half the morning especially if you have some calming mood music, scatter cushions and a couple of copies of Hello. Make it nice but not so nice they won't go out.

It is wise to set a check out time and make sure they know when that is. If you have stated 10.30am and they are still titting about in their room at 11, you will have to gird your loins, get up those stairs and kick them out – politely of course.

Try "Hi guys! Sorry to hurry you but the next guests have an early check in, and they are on their way!"

Usually the idea that other people are going to be tramping up the stairs to invade their space is enough to get them to hurry up.

There are some types who are not so easy to budge and these tend to be people who are nothing short of intimidating.

You might wonder why their direct, unblinking gaze sets off a chain reaction in your body. You might find yourself starting to sweat a little. There's a slight tremor in your voice and you have this terrible, overwhelming desire to please.

These people must surely remind you of your Maths teacher at school. A truly terrifying beast from the nightmare realms that was never satisfied with only biting off your head.

You MUST get a grip immediately. You cannot allow these guests to control your relationship right from the start, or basically you're fecked for the length of their entire stay. You won't sleep properly in your own bed because you are on red alert. If you are floppy at that first meeting, they will devour you and spit out the pips at breakfast.

And then there are the guests who will never be pleased with anything.. ever.

It is very important you do not take anything they say or do personally. Do not be affronted and feel bad. You are doing a fantastic job – even if you're not.

You might have someone come to the door and before you can crack a smile and utter a welcoming 'Bienvenue', they are already complaining.

It could have absolutely nothing to do with you or your premises, or your face. It could simply be there were no taxis waiting for them at the train station and the guest had to suffer the inconvenience of phoning for one.

When you get this type of person, identify them immediately and adjust your course accordingly. No matter what you do for this person they will complain.

You might have the most magnificent room (for the money) and they will tell you they had trouble plumping their pillows or pressing the knobs on the remote control.

You must resist the urge to either a) become a stroppy git and mentally tell them to eff off every time you see them, or b) turn into a blobby piece of slimy ooze who constantly tries to bend into a shape that they will like.

These people are half-empty people and they always will be.

It is best to pity them because their lives must be full of shit.

Attractiveness

This is a knotty problem and no mistake.

My recommendation is that you do not make yourself deliberately too attractive.

There is no need to go the other way and make yourself look like Worzel Gummidge or Theresa May, but go easy on the trimmings.

Don't go dolling yourself up like Joan Collins whoever you are – you will only confuse people.

This may go against the grain as most of us tend to be vain as cock birds, but I can tell you it can cause you major problems if you overload the aftershave and slick on that fire engine red lippy with too much enthusiasm.

People get the wrong idea so quickly.

It's quite alarming how simply showing someone a bedroom, smiling, being polite and courteous, telling them if they need you for anything just call, can be misconstrued as you running some kind of knocking shop and what time would they like their quickie?

It helps if you are over 50, but it won't save you if someone is determined (or possibly desperate).

It might be you have a gentleman stay from Australia. You get the first inkling that something is coming up when he enquires as to the whereabouts of your husband and if you are free this evening.

It is very important that you explain your situation with as much detail (true or false) as you can. Lay down the law immediately before he tries to lay anything else on you.

It can be tricky when cornered. Rooms generally only have one door in or out and if the interested party has that exit covered it can be difficult to manoeuvre yourself out of harm's way.

To hear how a gentleman's wife really *doesn't* understand him and how pleasant and kind you are, is a sure sign things are going the wrong way. Do not be lured by any attempts at flattery. It's a red traffic light – there is always an agenda.

I would suggest you never go right into a room with a new guest. Let them go in first and you hold your ground by the door. Be firm.

But not too firm - some wierdos love that sort of stuff.

Being adaptable

Things change all the time.

None of us ever know what's coming up next, no one can foretell the future - not even the vicar of St Mary's or Madame Cleopatra with her crystal balls.

Running a B&B means you need to be able to adapt yourself (and your fixtures and fittings) at a moment's notice.

Things happen when people are around, and these are often destructive things. Guests break stuff and stuff breaks all by itself.

Sometimes the hand of fate reaches down from the cosmos and turns off your electric hob 10 minutes before breakfast service. It's as dead as a dead door nail, it's not working, and you cannot cook anything.

You have to adapt to the changing circumstances in a flash, spring into action and find an alternative. The clock is ticking and the animals want feeding.

Diving under the stairs to look for your camping stove is an excellent solution. Yes, it's only got one ring, is perilously wobbly and absolutely stinks of gas, but you can do this, and do this you will.

Your guests will never know what you've been through when you serenely glide into the breakfast room with plates piled high with breakfast delights.

These are the kind of things that turn you into a B&B super hero.

You might get a gentle tap on your 'privates' from time to time with a request to sort out the basin in the bathroom.

The pop-up, pop-down plug has popped down and isn't having any of the pop-up.

Be careful here. If you rush too quickly to assist, you might not think to grab your marigolds on the way.

The sight of a sink full of brown scummy water with black curly hairs floating on the top could cause you to throw up in your mouth and regret your haste.

Think fast and try to talk your way out of it.

If that doesn't work you might have to take one for the team and plunge your hand in to the sink soup.

You can only hope you don't pick up anything too itchy and long term.

Some of us had to learn stuff the hard way – it's just the way it is – but a little foresight and a stout pair of rubber gloves can save you a nasty fungal infection.

La Vie Amoureuse (aka The Love Life)

Some people cannot control themselves, and even if they can they won't when they are on a weekend mini-break.

I have to say at this point that in my humble opinion a shag-athon should only take place in a Hotel. It's really not on to turn up to someone's home and make a porno movie.

Hotels are much more geared up for this kind of stuff.

No one gives two shits who you are.

Apart from when you book in, you never have to speak to anyone. The long suffering, under-paid staff who come in and clean up after you will never meet you or recognise you in the street. The whole business is completely anonymous, and that's how it should be.

Frankly to go at it like rabbits all night long in someone's family home and then come down to breakfast as if nothing has happened takes some bloody nerve.

But still they do it.

You might have to be prepared to turn a blind eye (and ear) to the activities of these types of guests.

After a few months of running your B&B, and if you are at all attentive, you can pretty much tell what's on the agenda as soon as this particular type arrives.

You might, for example, get a gentleman knock on the door, rather later in the day, and ask if you have a room. You might get an inkling that something is afoot when he tells you his girlfriend will be arriving shortly and that he will be back later on. And no, there is no luggage.

I would suggest, assuming you have a room and you want to let him have it, that you extract full payment in cash right away.

When the girlfriend turns up and seems not only considerably older than the gentleman but also has an air of weary worldliness about her, you begin to paint a picture of where this is going.

You may find you never actually see the gentleman again. This is because he doesn't return to the B&B (or his girlfriend) until after midnight and is gone again by 5am, thus missing out on an absolutely banging breakfast.

But then again perhaps he's had enough of banging.

As you serve the sausages in the morning, the girlfriend, who seems very relaxed and chatty at this point, tells you her life story. It's all very entertaining if not a little alarming.

Who knew?

How other people live their lives is a wonderful thing.

It reminds us of the diversity of life in all its different forms and how we must not shun alternative ways of being. Better to be open minded and open hearted I say.

We cannot know someone else's path and it is very wrong of us to judge them. Especially, as in this case, I for one have little knowledge of her particular field of expertise.

As this lovely lady devours the rest of her pre-paid breakfast, jingles her bangles and asks for more tea, it is perfectly possible this fascinating encounter triggers a response in oneself.

You could be completely mesmerised by this exotic lady and suddenly feel as frumpy, plain and taupe as it gets. Ones favourite fluffy slippers may begin to look a little shabby and there's the awful realisation that one's roots need doing.

When there is a pause in the spine chilling memoirs you might have the temerity to enquire as to the whereabouts of the absent gentleman. Do not be surprised if she merely shrugs her pretty shoulders and says "He's gone".

Because indeed he has, and that is why you must always, always, always take payment up front in these sensitive situations.

Needless to say, after she checks out and you go up to do the room, you will be requiring your marigolds again.

On another occasion it could be you have a young man turn up on his own who has booked well in advance. He does however have on his face what looks very much like an "eager beaver" expression.

He installs himself upstairs after saying that when the door bell rings he will answer it. You smile to yourself and retreat downstairs to your lair to await developments.

You don't have to wait very long.

'Ding dong!' goes the bell and you hear the young man launch himself from the top of the stairs in one giant leap for mankind and literally fly into the arms of his amour who is waiting on the doorstep.

"This is cute!" you hear her say as her heels click loudly on the woodblock flooring.

The young man less than gallantly bulldozes his 'cutie pie' up the stairs to their room.. before hurriedly closing the door.

"Yahoo!"

In the morning, after you have removed your earplugs, you are cooking the breakfast and realise the time is ticking by and the love birds are still not down.

Half an hour later, the bacon is carbon and it's still a 'no show', so you go to the bottom of the stairs to have a listen.

At that moment your other guests descend to the breakfast room looking a little disturbed. You make their tea, give them their brekkie and chat comfortingly about the weather.

Still no young man and gf, so you decide to go up and see what's what. Before you get a chance to knock on the door, you are regaled with such a grunting, moaning and squealing it sounds like the pigs have escaped the abattoir and are rampaging through the town.

You make the wise decision to leave them to it, go back downstairs and sling their breakfast in the bin.

When they leave a little later and drop off the key, you might find not a word is spoken.

It's best not to comment - even if you are dying to.

And don't forget your marigolds.

Bear in mind it's not always the young who partake of some afternoon (or early morning) delight.

Do not discount the grey and seemingly disinterested. They can be so vocal and appear to be in so much pain, it can leave you wondering whether to call an ambulance.

Trust

If you are a suspicious type who reckons everyone is on the make, you might find B&Bing rather arduous and stressful.

For one thing you have to give your guests a set of house keys.

Some keys are for their room of course but you also need to give them the keys to your very own front door.

Unless you are prepared to sit in the hall 24/7, eyes on the porch ready to repel all invaders, checking everyone in and out like the US border control, you are going to *have* to trust your visitors.

If you think everyone has an angle or is out to get you, this just might not be the best direction for you.

If you are not prepared, or able, to commit fully to this venture there could be problems ahead.

For example, if you happen to distrust your fellow man with a vengeance, and also happen to have a day job as well, it might be wise to make a choice between the two as there could be a conflict of interest.

Someone who keeps a baseball bat by the front door and has to be at their office desk by 9am is not going to get the best experience out of hosting.

Welcoming your guests in by squaring up to them and barking out the house rules is not a happy start. Rushing them through their painfully early breakfast and virtually throwing them out into the street is worse and will only get a person a bad name.

Such actions have been known to result in a host finding a drawer full of half eaten fish and chips festering in a bedside table.

People enjoy a bit of payback.

It is wise, therefore, to already possess a belief in the inherent goodness of people before you embark on this journey.

It is far better to have the assumption that most people are lovely – because they are.

Of course you are going to get the odd wanker, actually and metaphorically, but as a rule of thumb if you keep your prices not too high and definitely not too low your guests will turn out to be types who are appreciative of a lovely holiday in a nice place.

They will be happy not to get ripped off by you and probably be genuinely captivated by anyone who makes a living in the extraordinarily weird way you do.

This is also how you get to make some excellent bffs.

By sheer weight of numbers, you are bound to find someone you can be fond of. They might come from the Andes, Honolulu or Afghanistan, which makes popping round for a coffee a bit of a challenge - but love usually finds a way.

Very, *very* occasionally it can be earth moving, life changing, 'soul-mate' type stuff.

Once in a blue moon you will find yourself walking towards the front door and seeing through the glass someone who, like a blessed pilgrim, has come home.

There is nothing quite so magical as meeting a new person for the very first time, looking into their eyes and knowing somehow you already know them - and what's more they know you too.

When you talk to each other it's like a conversation you have always had in a place you have always been. People call it love at first sight, but it is so much more than that.

It's like Karma I think, or possibly fate, or its written in the stars, or it's like playing the lottery with enough tickets. In the end you are going to hit the jackpot.

Whatever it is and whenever it happens, you know to no longer believe the old lie that the right person will never come knocking on your door.

Trust me, it can happen.

Whether you get to keep them or not is another matter. Usually they belong to someone else and you have to give them back.

Sleep and Stamina

You don't necessarily need to be a thoroughbred to go this distance, but a bit of donkey DNA won't go amiss.

This work is hard if you are doing it all yourself. Going to the gym to beast yourself twice a week isn't going to help that much but you do need some level of fitness. Beds don't make themselves you know.

B&B is 24/7 and unless you can anticipate when you are going to succumb to the flu and shut the shop in advance, you are going to have to cope when you only want to be left alone to die.

Sadly, most guests don't give a flying arse how bad your dose of the runs is. They still want their bacon and they want it now.

If you are not well, it is really hard to scramble eggs, clean a shitty toilet and smile about it.

Some hosts I've known simply 'medicate' their way through a malaise. In other words they drink their way through it.

I don't recommend this, but then these days I'm a rubbish lightweight boozer whose drinking days are but a distant, slightly hazy memory. I think.

Answering the door in your pyjamas all swivel-eyed and slurring, reeking of Jack Daniels and mumbling the antibiotics aren't working is never going to get you 10 out of 10 on Tripadvisor.

There's no way round it unless you have loving friends and family prepared to step into the breach. You alone will have to find that extra mile in the tank no matter how many you already have on the clock and what demons are circulating in your blood.

Even if you are not that ill you can still get knackered, so 'early to bed' is a darn good motto. Stick it on your fridge.

One piece of advice for all new B&Bers. Try not to go out and have too much fun. You'll only regret it.

A hungover, wrecked proprietor may think they've got away with not having to do brekkie in the morning because they've told their guests they're sorry but they have a migraine (such a curse!). But they're only fooling themselves.

Guests have ears too and falling over the door mat at 2am, kicking the cat and swearing like a docker about having to cook another 'feckin' full English' in the morning will have given the game away.

When you 'early to bed' remember that means *go to sleep.*

Try not to be tempted to check emails, gamble the on-line lottery, frighten yourself half to death with depressing, distorted and usually inaccurate news reports, get lost in the status updates of people you don't even like on Facebook or play too many rounds of mahjong. These activities will only shorten your life.

Sometimes, however, there is literally nothing you can do. You *have* to stay up.

Sometimes a guest will say they want a check in later than normal. Let us say 9pm. That's not too bad is it? You can do that! Watch a bit of telly, cuddle the cat (perhaps not that), read about how Richard Branson made his fortune selling melons, and sip a cup of rooibos.

You might check the clock at 9.30 and pull a face, but it's not that late, it's still ok.

10 o'clock and the pulled face might have become a frown.

Where are they? Bed is beckoning and the telly gets scary after the watershed.

You decide to find the guest's mobile number and give them a call. It's hard to do this as you don't like hassling people, but needs must. You ring the number.. and there's no reply.

Alright, well perhaps they are outside unpacking the car right now and can't answer the phone.

You cock an ear for the doorbell, but all is silence.

A little later you hear your other guests come in and take the stairs to their room. Such a nice young couple.

Now its 10.30 and the frown has become a scowl. Where the dickens are they?

You try the mobile again and, god be praised, a voice says "Hello?"

"Oh hi, its Penny from the B&B" Immediately you hate yourself for falling into simpering politeness. "Just wondering where you are?"

"Oh, so sorry, I'm moving my daughter out of her flat and its taking longer than expected. We're going to catch the last bus back"

Bus? What bus?

"What time is the bus?" you enquire your heart sinking.

"About 11.30 I think"

You know these people are at least half an hour away, so at best it's going to be midnight before they get here. The lovely young couple upstairs want a 7 o'clock breakfast and the will to live is beginning to seep away.

You hear yourself say something about not holding them up any longer and you ring off.

Shit. Shit. Shit.

The clock drags its way round to midnight, your eyes are like sunken cesspools and if you weren't so tired you would be biting the heads off chickens.

It's midnight and no guests.

Where the fuck are they?

You phone again. No answer. You're not having any of it and you just keep ringing. In the end the same voice says "Hello?"

You remind them it is now midnight and they are still not with you.

"It's taking a bit longer than expected. We've missed the bus"

Genius.

So, when will they arrive?

"Nearly finished. We'll get a taxi"

One o'clock and you find you've fallen asleep in your cup of cold rooibos and now have a red ring on your face.

Fuck it, the bastards can sleep outside on the curb.

You get into bed and drift off into a fitful sleep. You dream about drowning hundreds of headless chickens in giant rooibos cesspools floating with melons.

Ding dong! Your heart literally stops beating.

It's 2.30 am and on the doorstep are two enormous ladies with what looks like an entire room full of junk. The taxi driver gives you a sympathetic grin and drives off to live another day.

Mum and daughter.

"Sorry – it took a bit longer than expected"

No shit, 6 hours longer.

By the time they are upstairs, they've faffed about, crashed about, visited the bathroom six times and finally fallen asleep its 3.30am.

Breakfast service commences in 2 and a half hours... Suck it up.

Leftovers and Hidden Costs

People leave parts of themselves behind all the time. Usually in the form of hair, faecal matter and used condoms, but sometimes you get things that are not just their DNA.

It won't be too long before you can open a branch of Superdrug.

Shampoos and shower gels are favourites followed by paracetamol, deodorant and nail polish.

You can open a branch of WH Smith with all the newspapers, publications, books, pens and magazines, but none of them are much good as the crosswords have all been done.

You can stay up to date with the European news and practice your French and German at the same time with copies of Le Monde and Die Zeit. But sometimes there are magazines you really only want to handle with your marigolds.

Very, very occasionally you might get money but not enough to open a bank or change your life.

You could open a charity shop with jumpers though, odd socks, shower caps and dirty pants, but a silver box full of dog ends might turn out to be your greatest treasure.

A bit of fore-thought can save you a lot of hassle and expense. When you show your room to your guests make sure they are listening.

Make sure you explain EVERYTHING about your B&B to your guests. How to use the key in the door, where the towels are and especially how to turn on a tap. Failing to do this could cost you dear.

For example, you might have some guests from the Swiss mountains who have never experienced a push and lift window latch or a lift and swing bathroom tap.

Leaving Heidi without proper instructions is only asking her to acquire unnatural feats of strength in order to get water out of the faucet and air into the room.

Finding after checkout that the bathroom tap designed for 180 degrees has been twisted through 360, and therefore rendering it as useless as a chocolate teapot, is nothing but one's own fault.

Forking out £150 for a new one is a painful yet effective reminder to be more mindful next time.

You can be grateful once again however, because on this occasion, even though she couldn't get the windows open, Heidi didn't asphyxiate herself or her partner as the trickle vents were open and kept them alive.

Support

You are going to need some mates, or at least a support group.

You will need someone on whom to off load when your crazy life gets a bit too crazy. Sharing with others helps you to know it's not just you who attracts all the oddballs and weirdos in life - your friends get their fair share too.

Nothing beats having a natter and a heart to heart with a real, live human being, and believe it or not B&B hosts are generally human. Although to be fair I've got my doubts about one or two I've met.

Getting together with other B&Bers can be like chicken soup - without the chicken. Quorn soup really – it's guilt free. You feel better just by thinking about it. Telling each other your B&B stories doesn't hurt your guests and can be better therapy than diazepam and prosecco put together – believe me I've tried.

This story from a friend of mine is a real doozee.

A single male guest slept off the effects of his 'night before', all day long while fully clothed on the top of his duvet. The men he was supposed to be supervising went off on their own to fit out a shop in town. Later that night, the man got up, went out and did it all it all again while his workers stayed in and got an early night. The man got absolutely plastered all over again, lost his keys, hammered on the B&B door at 2am, threw up in the herbaceous border, was refused entry, went off shouting abuse, got spotted climbing a drainpipe on CCTV, broke into the shop they were refitting, got arrested and was left to rot by his co-workers.

It's a classic.

Then there was another man who booked to stay a fortnight and said his company would pay the bill. But when the B&B host phoned them to get payment they said the man had stolen from them and was now wanted. Poor B&B host twisted fingers all night wondering what the hell to do.

At 8 am the following morning the door bell went and on the doorstep was the Old Bill. The guest's employer had phoned the police and told them where he was.

"Is he here?" they enquired.

"Yes!" replied anxious host "he's asleep but told me to wake him at 8.30."

"Don't worry about that – we'll wake him for you"

A few minutes later, the guest checks out in a very fetching pair of handcuffs.. and they weren't pink fluffy ones from Anne Summers.

One of my very favourite stories involves yet another single gentleman.

He stayed at my friends B&B every summer for years. He was a unique and interesting fellow as you are about to find out.

The B&B was situated only 10 minutes walk from the beach. You could wander down at your leisure and not need to worry about parking or anything boring like that. The little town had cafes and ice cream parlours to visit and one could have a lovely, peaceful break admiring the spectacular coastline with the soaring seagulls, crashing ocean waves and golden sands.

This particular gentleman would enjoy all of these things. But he had a very special way of doing it.

Every morning he would come down to breakfast stark naked apart from his speedos.

For those who are not acquainted with this particular form of gentleman's swimwear, may I explain that they are also colloquially referred to as 'budgie smugglers'. Do you get the picture? If not, I may have to draw you one.

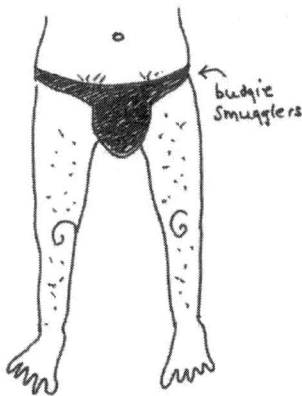

This informal attire at breakfast is fine if the speedo wearing guest is your only guest and you are partially sighted, but if you also have a family from Birmingham with two small children brought up to speak their mind, they are likely to point out the bleeding obvious.

The gentleman was generally oblivious to sniggers and smirks and would eat his breakfast in peace, get up and leave the table (Tee Hee! Look at that Dad!).

He would walk through the village and out onto the beach without so much as a hand towel to give the budgie some privacy. Once there he would lie down on the sand and remain in one place until the tide came in.

This is what he did year after year.. until one day.

After he had checked out, my friend went in to do the room, and there in the bin were his crumpled, well-worn speedos.

He never came back again.

You will have your own stories to tell, but like I said, be discerning and keep your prices right and they shouldn't be too hair raising.

How to get guests

Your B&B is going to be a bit of a flop if you don't have any guests.

As a rule of thumb it can take about 5 years to build up a business from scratch. You have to hang out a sign, advertise in relevant publications and wait for the doorbell to dong and the phone to ring.

Once one or two people have come, you can hope they will tell their friends, and they will tell their friends and so on.

If you are knocking on a bit this could seem a bit depressing. Time tends to take on a measure of importance when it starts to run out.

Fortunately, we live in the 21st century and at the time of writing we have a thing called the internet which can speed things up a bit.

In an afternoon you can put your glorious B&B out there to the whole world and get those bookings coming in.

There's so many places to pitch your gaff. Booking.com for instance, Expedia, Trivago and numerous other internet sites where anyone and everyone will get to know about you - and it's not too difficult to set it up. Even *I* managed to do it without screaming.

You can arrange for payment to be taken upfront by your website of choice so you don't even have to worry about all that nasty, dirty, filthy money business when your guests arrive.

If you should decide to take payment yourself, remember most people want to pay by card, and if you haven't got a card machine, it can cause some inconvenience and ill temper.

You might get some guests from South Africa who flatly refuse to pay with cash and want to give you a cheque. (As if!)

You might then have to explain that you cannot accept cheques and cash is what is required. You could helpfully suggest there is a hole in the wall, full of money, just over the road if your guest would care to go get some.

Unfortunately, it is possible that you could then be subjected to some rather unkind and intimidating words by a very large, angry man who says it's raining and he doesn't want to get wet.

Setting aside the urge to say something idiotic like "You might enjoy it!" or "It will do you good", or

"You're not a Furby are you?" you absolutely mustn't flinch. Under no circumstances cave in to this guest brutality.

As always you must stand your ground in these difficult circumstances and bullishly hand him your golfing umbrella.

If, when the money is grudgingly procured from the hole in the wall it is subsequently thrown in your face, try not to take it personally.

Accept you will get a crap review, put the money in your purse.. and move on.

Sometimes paying with cash can cause acute embarrassment even to you.

It could be the guest has requested a receipt, and unbeknownst to you has quietly followed you into your 'privates'.

While you are fully engaged writing out the receipt, it is exceedingly disturbing to turn and see the guest counting out the money on your unmade bed.

This kind of situation can make you blush like a 12 year old.

One thing to note if you are using one of the internet sites to build your business, is that it will cost you real money.

These sites take commission, sometimes more than 15%. (Blood sucking bastards).

The other thing they do is hold your money for up to 6 weeks before forwarding it on to you.

How do they do this and sleep at night?

It's easy for them. They are not people and therefore do not need to sleep. They are greedy money grabbing corporations with no soul, that's how.

It works like this..

Some sites pay hosts around the 15th of the month for the *previous* month's guests. So even though a guest might have been charged a week before they actually come and stay with you, if they don't check out until the 1st day of the following month, that money will rest in the website's account until the 15th of the month after that. Great little earner for them, wouldn't you say?

If you suck it up and let the resentment go (it may take a while), this still works very well and you will undoubtedly get far more guests than trying to go it alone.

It is important you take some professional photos of your place. Tidy up, put the loo seat down, make the bed properly - and *no effing teddies*.

Remember this will be the first time prospective guests get an idea of what they are paying for.

It's a good idea to include some pictures of your breakfasts, so try to make sure they don't look too much like Fido's dinner after the cat's had a go at it.

Add to the information pages all the wonderful things your guests can do nearby.

Beaches (if there are any), sites of special interest (ditto), cycle paths, walks, shopping centres, bars, cafes and restaurants. All the stuff you would like to do if you could only afford it.

Before you start your new life, make a decision about children.

Do you want any?

If you are over 50 it could be a bit late.

But what about other people's?

It's a risky business because kids do make such a feckin' mess. They can't help it. One little monster can redecorate your best guest room in an hour or less. They can scribble and tiddle and generally ruin everything you have worked so hard for.

However, if you love children (and most sane human beings do), you will also know how adorable they are, how much fun they are and how much joy they bring.

Personally speaking when it comes to your B&B business, screw all the above.

I *never* accept children.

But sometimes the little buggers get in under the radar.

For example, a couple might turn up at the door all smiles with their luggage in tow. All proceeding as normal until you notice there is a small person lurking near their car. You might draw your guest's attention to the child and enquire as to the owner.

When the guests announce they are "really sorry" but at the last minute they had to bring their son with them because the babysitter let them down – what do you do? Refuse them all entry? Direct the child to the kennel in the back garden and throw him a bone?

What are your realistic choices?

None whatsoever.

Sharp intake of breath, say it will be an extra £20 per night, and dive under the stairs for the camp bed.

Your fingers will be crossed for the entire length of their stay, hoping the child won't decide to take out his budding adolescent angst on your erstwhile pristine decorations.

Speaking of fearsome creatures, a word about dogs.

I love them, I really do. The owners can be a bit strange, but the dogs are lovely. However, I don't love them quite so much when they come in covered in mud and shake all over the wallpaper. I don't love them when they jump up and scratch my legs and slobber all over my trousers. I don't love them when they leap about all over the furniture leaving dirty paw marks as they go, and I particularly don't love them when they wee up the curtains and chew holes in my doors.

Therefore, it would be my strong recommendation to refuse dogs *and* their owners.

It's just so much extra work and you have to be mindful that future guests might be allergic to hairs and dog smell. Dogs bits get everywhere and keeping your space spotlessly clean is hard enough as it is.

Do yourself a favour and say 'Sorry, but no doggies'.

Once you have been up and running for a while your guests will start to leave reviews, and if they like you that will be a very good thing.

If they don't like you it will be disastrous. You are only ever as good as your last review and it's a dog eat dog world out there, so play nice.

Sense of Humour

If you haven't got one, you had better get one quick because this is where your salvation lies.

The ability to laugh at yourself, your guests, and the ridiculous, odd and downright weird things that happen will literally keep you sane.

Laughing about everything will keep you in the money and out of the asylum.

To see the cosmic joke will make all the work, the irritations, the inconveniences and the miles of ironing well worth it in the end.

You might get an epiphany and realise that your guests have come into your life for an extraordinary reason.

If you are open to it, and you allow it, they will literally show you *who you are.*

Guests are experts at highlighting every single phobia, neurosis, quirk and paranoia you have ever had. Their ways will haul out everything you've hidden from yourself (all that rage, jealousy, guilt and anger), and you can either laugh about it and learn from it - or miss the golden opportunity and go back to the boring old you (no offence).

Eventually you might come to bless every single one of these endlessly varied human beings that choose to come and stay with you.

In the end you may not judge yourself or others quite so much, because in this asylum we are all as mad as hatters and the sooner we realise that the better for everyone.

You could come to see that we are all unique and perfectly wonderful in our own way – even our guests.

But all the same, you will probably hope to God you never have to see them ever again.

And finally…

A Love and fascination for all things human.

Let's face it, if you don't like people run a cattery. If you don't like cats write a book.

It really is pointless to even consider running your B&B if you don't like people. Because people are what it's all about.

People are extraordinary. They come in all shapes and sizes, from different backgrounds, ethnic groups and cultures. They have different habits and beliefs, ideas and aspirations. Some like some things, and others loathe those very same things.

We are all different, valuable and worthy.

Running a little B&B will give you the opportunity to experience some of this amazing diversity that we are, and at the same time be reminded that deep down inside we all want pretty much the same things.

When someone comes from the United Arab Emirates and ignores your proffered hand, do not take offence. Go off and Google why that might be and realise there is no offence, only culture and tradition.

When someone ignores the plates on your breakfast table and eats off the mat, be gently amused while you clear up the crumbs. Its only humans being themselves in their own way.

If people should come and stay and after three days never have used the shower, don't judge them. Who knows what is going on for them.

To be a successful host means being able to not only accept the diversity of humanity but to also embrace it and sometimes even have fun with it.

Understanding and kindness counts and there isn't anyone on the planet who couldn't do with a little more.

From Melbourne to Moscow they will come to you. They will bring their old stories if you care to listen to them, and you and your little B&B will become one of their new ones.

Some will return time after time, but most will leave and you will never see them again. When those people hand over the key, jot a note in the guest book and say goodbye, you know that is the end of it.

Sometimes tears will come and there will be hugs and you will realise how much this experience has meant to them. A little part of you realises that something inside of them will always remember this.. and so will you.

To know someone's life has become a little more than what it was before because of something you have done and the way you have done it, must surely be worth all that goddam ironing.

The wonderful American essayist, poet and philosopher Ralph Waldo Emerson (1803 – 1882) says it all so much better..

"To laugh often and much;

To win the respect of intelligent people and the affection of children;

To earn the appreciation of honest critics;

To find the best in others;

To know one life has breathed easier because you have lived.

This is to have succeeded"

About the Author

Penny Edgar lives and works in Falmouth, Cornwall, UK and still runs her little B&B.

She is also a painter, photographer and illustrator.

Penny Edgar is a pseudonym (of course it is)

If you would like to get in touch with Penny you can reach her through her email:

auntiepenny@outlook.com

12220715R00066

Printed in Great Britain
by Amazon